T0368440

GEORGE W. DANIELS

and the

BROOKLYN BRIDGE

CHRISTOPHER J. DEE

AuthorHouse™
1663 Liberty Drive
Bloomington, IN 47403
www.authorhouse.com
Phone: 833-262-8899

This book is printed on acid-free paper.

ISBN: 979-8-8230-1887-6 (sc)
ISBN: 979-8-8230-1888-3 (hc)
ISBN: 979-8-8230-1853-1 (e)

Library of Congress Control Number: 2024904911

Print information available on the last page.

Published by AuthorHouse 05/29/2024

authorHOUSE®

GEORGE W. DANIELS AND THE BROOKLYN BRIDGE

George W. Daniels was born on April 15, 1866, at 49 Mott Street on the Lower East Side of New York. His mother, Mary Elizabeth Neumann, died soon after George was born.

In those days there were many ferries between the city of New York and the city of Brooklyn. Brooklyn was an independent city until its consolidation with New York on January 1, 1898. Boats carried people, horse trucks, and goods across the East River between the two cities. All around, steam engines on ferries smoked, bellowed, whistled, and pounded. Horse trucks and sailing ships were essential parts of the New York economy. The tallest building in New York at that time was Trinity Church.

The winter of 1866–1867 in New York was an extremely cold, rough winter. Ice clogged the river and kept the ferries idle for many weeks, and people walked across the frozen East River to the other side. Public demand to build a bridge across the East River became stronger.

On April 16, 1867, the New York and Brooklyn Bridge Company was incorporated by the New York State Legislature. The twenty-member board of trustees consisted of the mayors of New York and Brooklyn, the auditor and comptroller of the city of Brooklyn, eight trustees appointed by the mayor of New York, and eight trustees appointed by the mayor of Brooklyn. The board of trustees issued capital stock to fund the construction, oversaw the construction, hired the chief engineer, signed contracts, operated the bridge, and collected the tolls when the bridge was completed.

The Brooklyn Bridge was the first bridge between Long Island and Manhattan Island.

George Daniels's father was Michael Daniels. He was born in Clonmel, County Tipperary, Ireland, to Elizabeth Owen and Michael Sr., on November 15, 1833. His father died when Michael Jr. was a baby, leaving Elizabeth with Michael and two other sons, George and William. As a young man, Michael immigrated to the United States around 1850. His mother and both brothers immigrated to Australia shortly afterward. Michael had not learned to read and write—and perhaps this was true for the others too. And so they lost touch with one another forever.

During the Civil War, Michael took the place of a man about to be drafted, John D. Lake of Ramapo, Rockland County, New York State. Lake paid Michael Daniels a legally set fee of $700 cash, whereupon Michael went to Stony Point, New York, on September 30, 1864, and entered Company B, 69th Infantry Regiment of the Irish Brigade New York Volunteers. The wage was $33.33 for two months' service.

The 69th Regiment was at Skinner's Farm, Virginia, on March 25, 1865; White Oak Ridge, Virginia, on March 29–31; at the fall of Petersburg, Virginia, on April 2; Deatonsville Road, Virginia, on April 6; Farmville, Virginia, on April 7; and at the Appomattox courthouse on April 9, 1865.

Michael was there when Lee surrendered to Grant at the Appomattox courthouse. After that, he was honorably discharged near Alexandria, Virginia, on June 5, 1865.

Veterans' records indicate that Michael Daniels had blue eyes, brown hair, and a fair complexion and was five foot six in height.

After the war, Michael Daniels became an American citizen on September 13, 1869, at the Court of Common Pleas in New York County.

Michael worked as a laborer in New York City, where he lived at 370 Cherry Street. He was also a telephone pole installer and a farmer on Long Island in Farmingdale, New York.

On March 3, 1865, President Abraham Lincoln signed legislation establishing the National Asylum (later changed to Home) for Disabled Volunteer Soldiers. Initially there were three branches: the Eastern Branch in Togus, Maine; the Central Branch in Dayton, Ohio; and the Northwestern Branch in Milwaukee, Wisconsin.

Michael Daniels lived "out west" in the National Home for Disabled Volunteer Soldiers Central Branch in Dayton, Ohio. He was admitted there on June 4, 1903. The home had a strictly regulated military-style structure, and the men were required to wear uniforms. The US Army had a surplus of uniforms after the Civil War that the National Homes for Disabled Volunteer Soldiers used. When the surplus ran out, they continued to have new uniforms made. The veterans slept in barracks of about eighty, and they ate in large dining halls. The men helped construct buildings, care for the grounds, repair buildings, and care for the ill.

There were chapels for services and prayer meetings. They had farms where men worked. They sold some food, but they used most of it for the home. The men were able to earn some spending money through these programs. The home band had concerts and provided music for the daily raising and lowering of the flags. There were leisure activities, concerts, gardens, a zoo, and libraries. The libraries had books and newspapers donated by friends and family of the veterans. The Central Branch had more than twenty-five acres of flower gardens, and there were lakes for swimming and boating. Local people enjoyed visiting the beautiful grounds, gardens, and zoo. The Central Branch also had a small cave, a pond with an alligator, and a collection of wild animals, including a Rocky Mountain great bear, buffalo, and a monkey house. Also at the Central Branch, there was a cemetery that is now the Dayton National Cemetery. Some of the homes for Disabled Volunteer Soldiers evolved into Veterans Administration Medical Centers, and those that had cemeteries became national cemeteries.

In his later years, Michael suffered from heart disease and rheumatism. Only after persistent efforts was he finally awarded a federal disability pension of twenty dollars per month, beginning on February 23, 1909.

Michael Daniels went to visit his daughter Ruth Daniels Lumpe at 317 Hancock Street in Brooklyn, and he died there in his seventy-seventh year on May 15, 1910. He was on furlough from the "Old Man's Barracks" number 8. His son, George William Daniels, and his daughter Ruth buried Michael next to Mary Elizabeth Daniels in Mount Olivet Cemetery, in the Maspeth section of Queens, New York City. His grave is now marked by a Civil War veteran's monument provided by the Veterans Administration.

As a boy and a young man, George watched the construction of the Brooklyn Bridge.

The bridge's construction started on January 3, 1870, but the bridge wasn't completed until 1883.

John Augustus Roebling was the chief engineer of the bridge. He and his son Washington A. Roebling had designed and built several other bridges, including the John A. Roebling Suspension Bridge, which crosses the Ohio River from Cincinnati, Ohio, to Covington, Kentucky.

Before construction began, John crushed his foot, and they had to amputate his toes. Shortly thereafter, he died of tetanus, and Washington took over as the chief engineer. After Washington Roebling fell ill from caisson disease—now known as decompression sickness or the bends—his wife, Emily Warren Roebling, became a very important part of the construction of the bridge. She was the critical link between her husband at home in Columbia Heights and the engineers at the site.

Emily visited the construction site and gave directions to the builders. She had to convince the board of trustees that her homebound husband should continue to be the chief engineer.

In 1879, George left school after eighth grade when he was thirteen years old and took a job as an errand boy and then as a helper in a horse-feed concern. He got his first taste of the trucking business in September 1882, working first in the horse stable and then as a driver of a one-horse wagon and later a team of horses.

At that time, the horse was essential to New York City. Horses and horse-drawn equipment for transporting merchandise were the primary method of shipping. Horse trucks made deliveries of milk, ice, coal, beer, and all kinds of goods to homes and businesses throughout the city. City streets were crowded with single-horse and horse-team-pulled trucks, wagons, and carts used to haul goods.

George was a convert to the Catholic faith. At age fourteen, he was baptized on August 29, 1880, at St. Mary's Church on Grand Street in New York. His baptismal certificate lists Elizabeth Wilson as his mother and Bridget Cassin as his godmother.

Reading

Writing

Arithmetic

George's younger sister, Mary Elizabeth Daniels, was born in Farmingdale, Long Island, on April 26. 1861. She was a governess, and she lived with a family at the Hotel Abbottsford at the corner of West Thirty-Eighth Street and Sixth Avenue in New York. Governesses were usually in charge of teaching girls and younger boys. When a boy was old enough, he left his governess for a tutor or a boarding school. Traditionally, governesses taught the three Rs—reading, writing, and arithmetic.

On May 24, 1883, the Brooklyn Bridge was opened to traffic with a dedication ceremony. President Chester Arthur; Governor Grover Cleveland of New York; Franklin Edson, the mayor of New York City; Seth Low, the mayor of Brooklyn; the bridge trustees; Emily Roebling; and other elected officials and politicians were in attendance.

There was a prayer, speeches, and music from regimental marching bands, and ships in New York Harbor fired cannons. Emily Roebling was the first to travel across the bridge in a horse-drawn carriage. President Arthur led the first walk over the bridge. After the ceremony, elected officials went to a reception at the residence of Washington Roebling in Columbia Heights.

There was a toll to cross the bridge. According to American-Historama.org, "The initial charge to make the Brooklyn Bridge crossing was one penny to cross by foot, five cents for a horse and rider to cross and ten cents for a horse and wagon. The price charged for farm animals was five cents per cow and two cents per hog or sheep."

Walkers could buy books of twenty-five tickets for only a nickel for each book. By 1895, the walk was free.

George and his sister Mary Elizabeth walked across the Brooklyn Bridge. George was seventeen at the time of the dedication, and he had been working in the stable and driving horses for about four years.

The two cities employed street cleaners to remove horse manure from the streets. Horses created air contaminants harmful to health, noxious odors, noise, and horse manure and urine. City horses created millions of pounds of manure each day. Manure was collected into piles, and there were many, many flies—each one a spreader of germs. Manure dealers sold horse manure to farmers in Queens, the Bronx, Long Island, and New Jersey.

Mary Elizabeth Daniels, aged twenty-two and not married, died on September 22, 1883, at the Homeopathic Hospital at East Sixty-Seventh Street and Third Avenue. The cause of death was typhoid fever, and a contributing cause was pneumonia. Typhoid fever was spread in environments where feces came into contact with food and drinking water. There was a public health hazard associated with having horse manure in the streets.

P. T. Barnum and his elephants walked across the Brooklyn Bridge on May 17, 1884. Led by Jumbo, twenty-one elephants and seventeen camels crossed the bridge from New York to Brooklyn. P. T. Barnum wanted to promote his circus opening in Brooklyn and demonstrate that the bridge was strong and safe.

On June 1, 1884, George's older sister, Ruth Daniels, married Frederick Charles Lumpe at Saints Peter and Paul Church in Brooklyn.

In September of 1886, George W. Daniels joined Jackson Brothers, one of the largest trucking companies in New York City. They had their offices and a stable at 168 Church Street in Manhattan.

The firm was started by J. W. Jackson (Jacob Willets Jackson) and his brother B. A. Jackson (Benjamin Albertus Jackson). They owned a horse farm on Long Island of several hundred acres, near what is now the corner of Jericho Turnpike and Jackson Avenue in Syosset. When George joined the company, it operated twenty-eight horses.

The Statue of Liberty was a gift from France to commemorate the centennial of the Declaration of Independence. Americans built and paid for the construction of the granite and concrete pedestal, the base. The statue was delivered to New York and sat in 214 crates for over a year because they hadn't raised enough money to build the base. Joseph Pulitzer, the publisher of the *New York World* newspaper, helped out. He published the names of everybody who donated on the front page of his newspaper and gave out replicas of the statue to some donors. Schoolchildren collected pennies for this fundraiser. The *New York World* newspaper circulation increased tremendously, and finally enough money was raised to build the pedestal. The Statue of Liberty dedication was held on the afternoon of October 28, 1886. In the morning there was a parade that began at Madison Square and went by way of Fifth Avenue and Broadway down to the Battery at the southern tip of Manhattan. There was a detour so that the parade could pass by the World Building on Park Row. President Grover Cleveland, the former New York governor, was in the grandstand reviewing the parade. When the parade passed the New York Stock Exchange, traders were not happy, and they threw ticker tape from the windows. This was the first ticker tape parade.

In the afternoon there was a parade of ships and boats. The president and other dignitaries took a ship over to Bedloe's Island (now named Liberty Island) for the dedication ceremony. This ceremony was not open to the public. Later that night the torch on the Statue of Liberty was lit for the first time.

On Wednesday, November 23, 1887, George W. Daniels married Mary Donnan at the Transfiguration Roman Catholic Church in Brooklyn, New York. It was the day before Thanksgiving.

The following March was the Great Blizzard of 1888. Five years after it opened, the Brooklyn Bridge—the longest suspension bridge in the world at the time—was put to the test by one of the most severe storms in New York history.

On March 11, 1888, there was a relentless blizzard. The storm produced snow drifts of thirty to forty feet that went over the tops of houses. It took over a week to clear the snow. Fire stations were immobilized, and the cities of New York and Brooklyn were shut down. Rail transit was not possible for days, and telegraph infrastructure was disabled.

Hundreds of utility poles came down, and the downed wires presented a hazard to city dwellers. This hazard led to wires in Manhattan being buried.

Brooklyn was cut off from New York.

The newlyweds George and Mary lived in Brooklyn. At the time, George was a stable manager. There were about thirty-five horses in the stable in New York.

George walked across the Brooklyn Bridge during the blizzard to feed the horses.

He was a very hard worker and demanded a lot of himself.

In 1899, George became vice president of Jackson Brothers.

The change over from horse trucks to motorized trucks began around 1905 and was completed by 1929.

Along with J. Arthur Kennedy, George started Daniels and Kennedy in 1915.

George left Jackson Brothers in 1916. He had been with them for twenty-four years.

In March of 1918, J. W. Jackson and B. A. Jackson retired, and their company went out of business. They never had any motorized trucks.

In 1919, the United States Trucking Corporation bought out and merged the businesses of twenty-six of the largest trucking firms in Greater New York. As a result, it had more than two thousand employees, twenty-five hundred horses, and two thousand trucks.

On December 11, 1919, Daniels and Kennedy sold out their business for $132,695 cash and one thousand shares or $100,000 in stock of the United States Trucking Corporation. They agreed not to engage in the trucking business for ten years.

Daniels and Kennedy continued, however, to operate as a warehouse, garage, and realty business. When they sold, they had both horses and automobile trucks. They had 155 horses, 21 one-horse trucks, 28 two-horse trucks, harnesses, feed, stable equipment, blankets, pails, horse-truck covers, office furniture, and 9 motorized trucks. There were four 1918 Pierce Arrow trucks, four 1918 Packard trucks, and a 1917 Dodge runabout.

On February 14, 1924, federal agents made one of the largest liquor seizures in New York City. Prohibition agents raided the warehouse of Daniels and Kennedy at 558 Water Street and confiscated ten thousand cases of bootleg liquor. The agents were about to leave when suddenly the lights went out. They continued their search with lanterns and flashlights. The agents found a stairway leading to a trapdoor, which they forced open. Then the prohibition agents discovered a large storeroom with thousands of cases of liquor, empty bottles, labels, and equipment for the dilution of and bottling of liquor. J. Arthur Kennedy was released on a bond of $500 on a charge of possessing intoxicating liquor in violation of the Volstead Act.

Al Smith was born on the lower east side of Manhattan on December 30, 1873.

His father, Alfred, owned a small trucking firm.

On January 3, 1920, Al Smith became chairman of the board of directors of the United States Trucking Corporation.

In 1928, Al Smith was the Democratic Party's candidate for president, running against Herbert Hoover. After Smith lost the election, he became the president of Empire State Inc. and was involved in the construction and promotion of the Empire State Building.

George liked baseball. His favorite team was the New York Yankees, and he also followed the Brooklyn Dodgers and the New York Giants. He listened to baseball games on the radio and liked to go to Yankee Stadium and occasionally Ebbets Field and the Polo Grounds. He also liked to play cards, especially bridge.

On January 3, 1938, Daniels and Kennedy was back in the trucking business.

George was almost seventy-two years old when he returned to his trucking business.

George Daniels died at his home in Brooklyn on June 29, 1943, in his seventy-eighty year.

Al Smith died on October 4, 1944. George Daniels and Al Smith are both buried at Calvary Cemetery in Queens, New York. The graves are in First Calvary, Section 45, near each other.

George was, above all else, a family man. He taught his family the importance of being honest in their work and doing the best job that they could. He was not one to sit still too long and was a very driven person. He had a strong work ethic, and he was a perfectionist who would drive other people crazy.

In 1919, he purchased a townhouse in Brooklyn on St. Marks Avenue (#666), near Nostrand Avenue. This three-story house was faced in granite and had six bedrooms.

George took care of his wife and her family. He lived with his wife, his daughter, his brother-in-law, and two sisters-in-law. One sister-in-law was a widow, and her daughter also lived there in his home.

After the stock market crashed on October 29, 1929, his son, William, lost his job at the Corn Exchange Bank. Five months later, George's daughter-in-law, Florence, passed away suddenly. George welcomed William and his three children into his home. In the fall of 1930, George sent his two grandsons off to LaSalle Military Academy, a Catholic boarding high school on the south shore of Long Island.

His faith provided hope and strength and helped him overcome the difficulties and challenges of life. George and Mary had two children who died when they were very young. Robert was eight months old when he died on October 6, 1892. Marguerite was eighteen months old when she died on June 14, 1902.

Obituary

Transport Topics
Monday July 05, 1943
page 2 Weekly Print Edition

George W. Daniels Dies;
N.Y. Trucking Leader
In Business 61 Years

Veteran of Horse and Motor
Periods Held Many High
Posts in Councils of
Carrier Industry

New York—"During my years since '82, I have had the pleasure of working from the stable floor to the executive desk of the largest operations in the horse or motor periods in the great city of New York. With some pleasure, many headaches, and with good conduct, I hope to continue for several years among the many friends I have made."

Thus, early in 1938, spoke George W. Daniels on the occasion of the formation of the trucking firm of Daniels & Kennedy, Inc., and his installation as executive vice president.

Last week, the "many friends" of this veteran of 61 years of teamster and trucking operations learned with profound regret that he had passed away at his Brooklyn N.Y., home at the age of 75. He succumbed to an intermittent heart ailment which he had fought for some six months.

Was Director in ATA

As befitted a man entitled in every respect to the designation of "trucking expert," Mr. Daniels at the time of his death was a director of American Trucking Associations, Washington, D.C.; the New York State Motor Truck Association; and the Merchant and Truckmen's Bureau of New York. He served twice as president of the latter organization. He was also a member of the Traffic Club.

Not only was he a leader in highway transportation in his community, but the pioneer operator also held national prominence.

His experience and wisdom received recognition in 1929 when he served on a national committee appointed by the Secretary of Commerce to consider relief of traffic congestion. In 1930, Mr. Daniels was a member of a sub-committee named by the Merchant's Association to study problems arising from loading and unloading of trucks in narrow city streets. Later, during the life of the National Recovery Administration, his talents again were utilized as chairman of the New York City Code Authority for the trucking industry.

Mr. Daniels' career had an Algeresque touch in that he began literally at the bottom and worked his way right to the top. In doing so he participated in development of motor transportation from the earliest of the one-lung, boiler-type trucks.

Began at $12 a Week

Back in September, 1882, at the age of 14, Mr. Daniels began driving a horse and thus placed his foot on the first rung of the ladder to success. "Within a year," he once related, "I drove a team for the large sum of $12 per week for longer hours than when team drivers earned $36 per week without stable work on Sundays or holidays."

As gasoline engines replaced horse-power and the trucking industry came into being, Mr. Daniels took another step upward in joining the firm of Jackson Brothers, of which he eventually became vice president. Later, he and J. Arthur Kennedy formed the partnership of Daniels & Kennedy, with offices on Water Street.

When the United States Trucking Corporation was organized, the partners sold their business to it, with Mr. Daniels becoming vice president of the new company.

Early in 1938, however, saw the two going back into business for themselves under the title of Daniels & Kennedy, Inc., with Mr. Daniels taking the executive vice presidency he held up to his death.

The veteran operator leaves a widow; Mary A. Daniels; a son, William J.; a daughter, Libbie Daniels; and three grandchildren.

Mary Donnan Daniels (b. May 5, 1867; d. November 9, 1944) and George W. Daniels (b. April 15, 1866; d. June 29, 1943) had four children.

William J. Daniels (b. March 19, 1889; d. May 24, 1956)
Robert Daniels (b. February 7, 1892; d. October 6, 1892)
Mary Elizabeth "Libbie" Daniels (b. May 4, 1894; d. April 10, 1989)
Marguerite Daniels (b. December 1, 1900; d. June 14, 1902)

Katherine Daniels (b. 1810 in Ireland; d. January 30, 1895) and Margaret Daniels (b. March 1815 in Ireland; d. July 21, 1866) were already in the United States when Michael arrived.

They are all buried in Calvary Cemetery.

George had two sisters.
Ruth Daniels Lumpe (b. November 15, 1860; d. March 28, 1940)
Mary Elizabeth Daniels (b. April 26, 1861; d. September 22, 1883)

Ruth and Frederick Lumpe (b. February 1, 1861; d. January 14, 1940) are buried with the Sprague family in the Greenfield Cemetery, Uniondale, New York.
Samuel Sprague (b. 1804; d. December 2, 1891) and Catherine S. Sprague (b. 1820; d. June 6, 1905) took care of Ruth when she was a child.

Ruth and Frederick had five children—Raymond, Libbie, Edna, Carrie, and Clara. Raymond worked as a truck driver for Daniels and Kennedy.

Jacob Willets Jackson (J. W. Jackson) (b. January 24, 1858; d. December 30, 1936) and Benjamin Albertus Jackson (B. A. Jackson) (b. October 8, 1859; d. May 19, 1924) are buried in the Jericho Friends Burial Ground in Jericho, New York, near the Milleridge Inn.

John Arthur Kennedy (b. 1888; d. September 20, 1946) is buried in Green-Wood Cemetery Brooklyn New York.

Printed in the United States
by Baker & Taylor Publisher Services